Little Gems

Felicite Shulkin

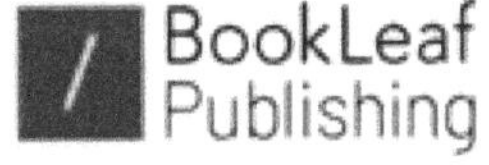

BookLeaf Publishing

Little Gems © 2022 Felicite Shulkin

All rights reserved.

No part of this publication may be reproduced, stored in a retrieval system, or transmitted, in any form or by any means, electronic, mechanical, photocopying, recording or otherwise, without the prior written permission of the presenters.

Felicite Shulkin asserts the moral right to be identified as author of this work.

Presentation by *BookLeaf Publishing*

Web: www.bookleafpub.com

E-mail: info@bookleafpub.com

ISBN: 9789357210843

First edition 2022

DEDICATION

I could not have gotten here without the support of my family and friends. Both have served as inspiration and laughter, and I am grateful to both.

ACKNOWLEDGEMENT

Thanks to BookLeaf publishing for creating the opportunity

Drumroll

The beat of the drum is steady,
Keeping pace with the way she sways.
A phoenix rising, you could see her
Wings set ablaze. She takes flight,
Turning black and white
Into technicolor.
Her eyebrows arch as she smirks
In cheeky defiance of the boundaries she breaks.
And as the drum roll rises in anticipation,
She laughs…
This chapter of hers has taken flight.

Unscripted

She stepped into the sun
And the warmth felt real
For the first time in years.
After a lifetime of being spoken
For, she finally became unscripted.

Microaggressions

She hid her face from the bright eyes
Of the sharks surrounding her.
They smelled the rich blood of a force
To be reckoned with, and did their best
To rip at her piece by piece. They
Took credit for her voice, discarded her thoughts,
And attempted to destroy the unique perspective
That would help her change the world.
They took everything they value in
Her, except the very thing that makes her
Valuable. They cant take her vision. They
Cant take the fire that burns within her to create
A better world.

Silk Sheets

Her skin becomes enveloped in
Evergreen silk sheets.
As she breathes in the sun,
She begins to feel.
Memories… Hope…
Anticipation lies at the tip of
The fingers that shade glittering
Eyes, so she could see the bright
light that shines and creates happiness
In the brisk springtime air.

Voices; compartmentalized

You can hear it in his tone
When he speaks with someone
Else. Private comfort with a
Loved one; the willingness to
Listen to a professional he respects.
His demeanor changes and in the
Second his shoulders slump
you see the layers of human he hides behind.
the silver tongue and steely wits are merely
Weapons he takes to battle every day.
For a moment, you sympathize with the man
He shows himself as. The way he compartmentalizes
The voices at his disposal, the parts of himself
That make him whole, you find you'll never
Really know what he's thinking. Just enough
To keep your distance. Just enough to trust him
With your life.

Keyboard Cruelty

It's easy, these days, to hide behind the keys at your
fingertips.
Friendships become battlefields as you arm yourself
with
A lifetime of disappointment and a face kind enough
to fool 'em.
And as you sit in the comfort of your own home,
where
Anonymity is ideal, and the possibility for an alibi is
real, you type the
Cruel words you tell yourself, in hopes that by
dragging them down,
You come out as queen of your own underworld.

Small reminders

My favorite flowers bloom in Winter.
They are no extraordinary pieces of art
But rather, they seem to go unnoticed.
That is, of course, until I pass by them
And catch a whiff of their honied scent.
I stop and smile at the memory they
Let me cherish. Yes, they're nothing
Much to look at, but they are the very
Reminders I need. Reminders of the
Little gems and childish dreams that
We convince ourselves to forget.
Within one whiff lays the hope that
One day, we will have time to commit
To these lovely whims again.

Weaponized

You trained me.
Made me the weapon of your choosing.
You never thought
I'd be your undoing.

Villains

Its an elaborate plan:
To create a space for love
With ulterior motives.
To play the hero with such
Malicious intent. To wear
Such shining armor, one
Can only barely see
The sharpened pins it's
Made of. Yes, its wonderful
Enough, until your mask's
Removed, and you become
The weakest villain in my
Storybook

Words

The Chinese alphabet is made of characters,
Not letters. Each character, each word,
Each phrase then develops a story of it's own
To tell. You write them down and they flow with
Emotion to truly honor the author.

Arabic and Hebrew letters create animated
Fluidity on each page they live on. These
cultures, their prayers are not just spoken
but sung to celebrate the miracles they
Were given.

Spanish… French… branded love languages
With poetic lilts in their tones. Conversations in
Native tongues like these arouse passion, arouse
Sentimentality, and yet the use of these languages
Find you chastised for their knowledge

Each language is created with beauty in it's strokes.
Each flourished word and folk story, each passionate
whisper
Leads to something great, some common ground, and yet
here we are,
Disregarding each other as if our languages and cultures are
our sharpest
barriers. As if our actions mean less because of our
culture's beliefs.
Our words turn cruel when we fear what we don't
understand,
And we forget that words are only words until they break
us.

Unlocked Memories

As fog sets in on this stretch of land,
The distant scent of fire makes its presence known.
It smells of sweets and strongly spiced cider
And memories of years gone by.
We were free then. Young and safe from the double-edged
Sword adulthood holds. Echoed laughter ends
The silence that I come home to. Vivid images
Of mischievous smiles swiftly return to make sure
I know this time did exist.
This was real.
These unlocked memories are the childhood ideals
We dream for.

Silent Hills

Shrouded behind thickening clouds are the mountains
surrounding this city.
It is now when everything seems most deserted, a
town laid to waste
In a horror flick, and yet… this is my favorite time of
day. The clouds are filled
With water, diluting the colors of another beautiful
sunset and asking me to be
A part of the pastel painting taking place. So I look
up to the sky, now darkening
By the minute and releasing droplets of water to the
ground, raise my arms up,
Arch my back, and smile. These silent hills are
heaven… collectors of souls…
Protectors of the earth they sit upon.

Whispers

Close your eyes and listen intently.
Bold and beautiful things are whispered
When the world becomes loud and
Attempts to distract you from your vision.

Indispensable

What you know. What you learn.
 It's the difference
Between becoming indispensable
And disposable.

Fernweh

I miss the texture between my fingers
Of a type of fiber, I've never felt. It's
Gentle skin moves like water, and a
Color so beautiful it has yet to be named.
It smells of honey and saffron, and some
Kind of spice that has yet to be found.
This very texture reminds me of home.
It's a home I have yet to live in, that I'm not
Quite sure exists, and here I am, eyes
Tightly shut, longing for what has yet to
Be created as if it's out there, waiting for
Me to find my way to it.

Four In The Morning

Waking up wide eyed in the middle of the night,
Still breathing and yet not taking a breath.
Fingers and toes curl animalistically,
As you wait for the attack to come. But there
Is no fight tonight. No reason to protect yourself
From sleep. And so, you turn to the torrential
Downpour of hot water. It becomes white noise
To drown out sound, and the accompanying steam
White light to drown out the darkness. Lemon balm
And mint whisk away the demons that tried to catch
You, and brings you back to calm.

Saved

In every moment he looks me in the eye and tells me
to be safe
        Or she offers fruit or a pot of tea.
Anytime they leave me be except for every kind word
they could think to speak,
        I feel safe. As if Ive been saved.
He smiles when I bring something for him
        While we all laugh at old jokes.
And reminisce about the nights we saw the sun rise,
and fell asleep with a grin.
        Each time I was saved by the mere
presence of friends.

Little Gems

Little cups of gelato on Summer's hottest day
Sit on a bright blue table.
It's sweetened cream glistens against the bright
Sun, and a breeze moves the flaps of
Colorful umbrellas. The patrons of the parlour sit
Outside in their white peasant blouses and their
Cream toned linen pants, and they're smiling.
They're embracing the little gems of today,
Letting their hearts brighten up in a way
That theyll cherish in the silent moments
Of gloomy day